Web Developers at Work

Careers in Computers

Corina Jeffries

COMPUTER SCIENCE For the REAL World™

Rosen Classroom™

Published in 2018 by The Rosen Publishing Group, Inc.
29 East 21st Street, New York, NY 10010

Book Design: Jennifer Ryder-Talbot
Editor: Caitie McAneney

Photo Credits: Cover ProStockStudio/Shutterstock.com; p. 5 Uber Images/Shutterstock.com; p. 6 Georgejmclittle/Shutterstock.com; p. 9 Timofey_123/Shutterstock.com; p. 10, 16-17 Monkey Business Images/Shutterstock.com; p. 13 Robert Kneschke/Shutterstock.com; p. 14 ronstik/Shutterstock.com; p. 18 Rawpixel.com/Shutterstock.com; p. 21 baranq/Shutterstock.com.

Library of Congress Cataloging-in-Publication Data

Names: Jeffries, Corina.
Title: Web developers at work: careers in computers / Corina Jeffries.
Description: New York : Rosen Classroom, 2018. | Series: Computer Kids: Powered by Computational Thinking | Includes glossary and index.
Identifiers: LCCN ISBN 9781508137757 (pbk.) | ISBN 9781538324424 (library bound) | ISBN 9781538355428 (6pack) | ISBN 9781538352748 (ebook)
Subjects: LCSH: Web site development--Vocational guidance--Juvenile literature. | Web sites--Design--Vocational guidance--Juvenile literature.
Classification: LCC TK5105.888 J44 2018 | DDC 006.7023--dc23

Manufactured in the United States of America

CPSIA Compliance Information: Batch #WS18RC: For Further Information contact Rosen Publishing, New York, New York at 1-800-237-9932

Table of Contents

What Is a Web Developer?

Do you like to work on computers? Are you a creative person? A career as a web developer might be your dream career!

Think of the last website you visited. In many cases, a web developer **designed** and created that website. They made sure the website was user-friendly, easy to find, and running smoothly. Web developers are responsible for the **technical** parts of the website. They know how to apply coding knowledge to the process of creating a website and making it perform effectively. As the Internet becomes more crowded with websites, jobs for web developers are on the rise.

If you know how to code, you're on your way towards a career in computers!

Web developers ask themselves what the website needs to achieve. Is it a newsletter? Is it an online store? Is it educational?

Web Experts

What do your favorite websites look like? What kind of information do they give? How are they useful, fun, or necessary? Maybe your favorite website has information about wild animals, and it includes pictures, facts, and videos. Maybe your favorite website has games and quizzes to help you study science.

Web developers are Internet **experts**. They know what makes an educational website successful. They know what makes an online shopping website successful, too. Web developers also know how to manage online traffic. They want their website to be visited and used by many people. Web developers take a challenge and find the best solution.

Learn a Language

Web developers have to speak more than one language. That's true for computer languages, anyway. Computer languages are ways to "speak" to a computer and get it to do a certain task. There are many different computer languages in use, such as JavaScript, PHP, and JAVA. Computer programmers and web developers use different languages for different tasks.

Web developers have to be very comfortable with the computer language they use. They have to "speak" very clearly to the computer to command it to do something. Good communication with a computer results in a successful website or program.

Unless you know the computer language, computer code looks very confusing.

Some people gain advanced degrees in computer programming, web programming, and computer science.

Go to School

Learning a computer language is one of the first steps towards a career as a web developer. What's another step you could take? Go to college!

Many web developers have a college degree. A two- or four-year degree is usually all that is necessary. There are degrees in computer programming and web programming at many colleges and universities. Other places offer "boot camps" that teach people how to code using the newest technology. In some cases, people are self-taught coders. If they keep up with the newest technology and can prove their skills, then they might get a job without a degree.

Create Something!

Another step for getting into the business of web development is to create something. Just as an artist or designer puts together a **portfolio**, an **aspiring** web developer should have something to show possible employers.

You can use your coding skills to develop a website. Make it something you're excited about and something that will show off your skills. You can do it for fun or volunteer to make something for a cause you're interested in. When you're applying for jobs, you can show employers your project. If it is a successful website or web application, then the work will speak for itself.

Portfolios and sample projects are great ways to show employers your style and skills.

Web developers often ask for feedback on their websites before they go live, or become available for use. Then, they **adjust** the website to make it better.

On the Job

Imagine you've taken all the steps to be hired as a web developer. What will the job actually look like?

Web developers spend a lot of time talking to customers to see what kind of website they want. Then, with that information, they can start building a website that fits the **criteria**. They may write and design the text and **visuals** of the webpage, or have web designers do those jobs. Web designers are experts of the visual side of websites. Web developers also have to test their websites to make sure things are working correctly. They make sure the website can handle many users at once.

Working with Customers

Web developers need to be masters of communication. They have to communicate with the computer through a programming language to build a website. However, they also need to be able to communicate with customers.

Web developers have to be able to listen to the ideas of their customers and make something they'll be happy with.

Companies, organizations, schools, and government agencies hire web developers to create their websites. Customers know what they want the website to achieve, but often don't know the technical steps to build it. Web developers must be able to explain technical problems and challenges to a customer in a simple way. The relationship with the customer may be long-term because websites need to be **maintained**.

Do you like to learn about the latest technology as soon as it is released? You might like to be a web developer!

Always Learning

A job as a web developer is not likely to be boring. For one, there are very many customers looking for help from a web developer. Another reason is that the field of web development changes all the time.

You may have learned one technique for building a website or one coding language. However, web developers need to be able to learn new techniques and languages as soon as they're created. This means staying on top of the latest technology at all times. Web developers have to be open to learning new things and acquiring new skills.

A Similar Career

What if you like the idea of creating websites but don't want to be a web developer? You might enjoy a career as a web designer.

Web developers tend to be more technical and **analytical** and they often focus on the parts of the website users don't see. Web designers are usually very artistic and creative. They have a vision for how a website should look. Web designers often work with a website's front end, or what the users see. They make decisions on colors, logos, and other **graphics**. Their job is to present website content in the best way possible.

Web designers need to be creative in their job every day!

Computer Careers

Web developers are in a quickly growing field. They are needed in many **industries**. In 2014, it was reported that web developers make an average of around $63,000 each year.

Careers in computers are quickly growing as new technology is created. Fifty years ago, a job as a web developer didn't exist. Who knows what careers in computers might exist someday? If a career in computers sounds like a good fit to you, make sure to stay on top of new computer trends and technologies. Find fun ways to learn and apply useful coding and computer skills!

Glossary

adjust: To make something better.

analytical: Of or relating to the ability to separate something into its parts or elements to better understand it.

aspire: To seek to accomplish a particular goal.

criteria: A standard on which a judgment or decision may be based.

design: The plan for how something should look.

expert: Someone with great knowledge about a certain subject.

graphic: A picture that represents or illustrates something.

industry: The businesses that provide a particular product or service.

maintain: To keep in good condition.

portfolio: A selection of a person's work collected over a period of time.

technical: Having to do with special knowledge about machines or instruments.

visual: Something, such as a graphic, that is used for effect or illustration.

Index